UEFA CHAMPIONS L[

300 QUESTIONS ON PLAYERS, TEAMS, TROPHIES & LOTS MORE TO TEST YOUR KNOWLEDGE

By
QuizGuy

UEFA CHAMPIONS LEAGUE QUIZ: 300 Questions on Players, Teams, Trophies & Lots More to Test Your Knowledge © 2020 by QuizGuy. All Rights Reserved. No part of this publication may be reproduced or transmitted in any form or by any means, electronic, mechanical, including photocopying, recording, or any other information or storage and retrieval system, without the permission of the publisher.

Also, in the series...

Preface

"To win the Champions League is huge for everyone."

Mohamed Salah

"The Champions League, for me especially, is the most beautiful competition."

Patrice Evra

"The Champions League is where the best players in the world come together."

Iker Casillas

"I believe the Champions League has all that magic because it gathers all the best European teams."

Neymar Jr.

The UEFA Champions League was rebranded in 1992, it was and still is also known as The European Cup. The European Cup was founded in 1955. Since becoming the UEFA Champions League, the competition has flourished and has provided entertainment and nail-biting moments year after year. The UEFA Champions League is known by many as the greatest competition in club football and it is the pinnacle of many professionals' careers to lift the trophy.

The UEFA Champions League Quiz is engaging and informative and will provide hours of entertainment for all of those who love this competition. The quiz will focus mainly on the competition since it became the UEFA Champions League in 1992, however there will still be some questions regarding the all-time records of the European Cup.

Hopefully, the quiz will remind you of some of the incredible talents that have graced this fantastic competition over the years.

QuizGuy has designed a quiz to test your knowledge on the UEFA Champions League. The quiz consists of 20 rounds each made up of 15 questions. You will be tested on lots of different topics related to player records, statistics, trophies, and lots more.

Now is the time to put your knowledge to the test! Good Luck!

Please remember this quiz is testing your knowledge on the Champions League which started from 1992. So, the questions will be from 1992 onwards. Unless the round says otherwise.

Table of Contents

Round 1: All Time Team Records (1955 – 2020) 1
    Round 1 Answers 3
Round 2: Champions League Teams Trivia 4
    Round 2 Answers 6
Round 3: Managers 7
    Round 3 Answers 9
Round 4: Player Records 10
    Round 4 Answers 12
Round 5: Hat-tricks, 4 goals & 5 goals 13
    Round 5 Answers 15
Round 6: Finals 16
    Round 6 Answers 18
Round 7: Goalkeepers 19
    Round 7 Answers 21
Round 8: Defenders 22
    Round 8 Answers 24
Round 9: Midfielders 25
    Round 9 Answers 27
Round 10: Forwards 28
    Round 10 Answers 30
Round 11: Comebacks 31
    Round 11 Answers 33
Round 12: Amazing Goals 34
    Round 12 Answers 36

Round 13: Memorable Moments 37
  Round 13 Answers 39
Round 14: Managers 2nd Round 40
  Round 14 Answers 42
Round 15: Final Locations 43
  Round 15 Answers 45
Round 16: Defenders 2nd Round 46
  Round 16 Answers 48
Round 17: Midfielders 2nd Round 49
  Round 17 Answers 51
Round 18: Forwards 2nd Round 52
  Round 18 Answers 54
Round 19: Penalty Shootout Trivia 55
  Round 19 Answers 57
Round 20: Challenging Trivia 58
  Round 20 Answers 60
Congratulations! 61

Round 1: All Time Team Records (1955 – 2020)

1. Which team has won the Champions League/European Cup the most amount of times?

2. Which team has finished runners-up in the Champions League/European Cup the most amount of times?

3. Only one Scottish team has ever won the Champions League/European Cup. Can you name the team?

4. Which club has lost the most amount of Champions League finals without ever winning the competition? The club in question, have been in the final on three different occasions but have lost in every one of those finals.

5. Which club is the most successful English team in the history of the competition?

6. Can you name the three teams from the Netherlands that have all won either the Champions League or the European Cup?

7. Only one French team have won the competition. Can you name the team?

8. A Greek team has only reached the final of the competition once. Which team from Greece was it that reached a final?

9. Which two English teams have a 100% record in Champions League/European Cup finals?

10. One German team has won five European Cups/Champions Leagues. Which team is it?

11. Which club is the most successful Italian team in the history of the competition?

12. Two Portuguese teams have both won the competition twice. Can you name the two Portuguese teams?

13. Which club is the most successful team from the Netherlands in the history of the competition?

14. How many times have Barcelona won the competition?

15. A Swedish team has only reached the final of the competition once. Which team from Sweden was it that reached a final?

Round 1 Answers

1. Real Madrid
2. Juventus
3. Celtic
4. Atletico Madrid
5. Liverpool
6. Feyenoord, Ajax and PSV
7. Marseille
8. Panathinaikos
9. Nottingham Forest and Aston Villa
10. Bayern Munich
11. AC Milan
12. Benfica and Porto
13. Ajax
14. Five times
15. Malmo FF

Round 2: Champions League Teams Trivia

16. The group stage starts after the preliminary rounds. How many teams are in the Champions League group stages?

17. Which team won the first Champions League in 1993?

18. Who are the current Champions League champions after winning the competition in 2019?

19. Which club has been the most successful in the Champions League era? The team in question have won the competition seven times since it became the Champions League.

20. Which team has lost the most Champions League finals?

21. A German team beat Legia Warsaw 8-4, which is the highest scoring game in the Champions League group stages. Can you name the German team?

22. Which English team has been involved in two 4-4 draws? One was with another English team and the other was against Ajax.

23. Only one club has successfully defended the Champions League title by winning it the following season. Which club has achieved this?

24. Which team has defeated Manchester United in two Champions League finals?

25. Which two teams have lost two consecutive finals in the Champions League?

26. Only one Ukrainian team has reached a Champions League semi-final. Can you name the team?

27. How many times have Arsenal reached the Champions League final?

28. Which three teams have won the Champions League having lost the final in the previous season?

29. Which two teams played in the only all Italian final in the Champions League in 2003?

30. Who two teams played in the only all German final in the Champions League in 2013?

Round 2 Answers

16. 32 teams
17. Marseille
18. Liverpool
19. Real Madrid
20. Juventus
21. Borussia Dortmund
22. Chelsea
23. Real Madrid
24. Barcelona
25. Juventus and Valencia
26. Dinamo Kyiv
27. One time
28. AC Milan, Bayern Munich and Liverpool
29. AC Milan and Juventus
30. Bayern Munich and Borussia Dortmund

Round 3: Managers

31. Which two teams has Jose Mourinho won the Champions League with?

32. One manager took charge of 190 games in the Champions League which is a record for a manager. Can you name the manager?

33. Which two managers have won the Champions League three times?

34. One manager has lost three Champions League finals which is a record for a manager. Can you name the manager?

35. Who is the youngest ever manager to win the competition? He won it at 38 years and 129 days.

36. One manager has coached 8 different teams in the Champions League. Who is the manager?

37. All the managers that have won the Champions League have been European. However, three non-European managers have been losing finalists. They all come from the same country. Which country is it these three managers come from?

38. Which two teams has Jupp Heynckes won the Champions League with?

39. Ottmar Hitzfeld won the Champions League twice with a different club each time. Which clubs did he win the competition with?

40. Can you name the two teams that Arsene Wenger has managed in the Champions League?

41. Louis van Gaal managed four different teams in the Champions League. Which team did he manage for the least amount of games in the competition?

42. Which two clubs has Massimiliano Allegri managed in the competition?

43. Which manager led Liverpool to glory in the Champions League in 2019?

44. Fabio Capello won the competition one time as a manager. Which team did he win the Champions League with?

45. Which club did Rafa Benitez win the Champions League with?

Round 3 Answers

31. Porto and Inter Milan
32. Sir Alex Ferguson
33. Carlo Ancelotti and Zinedine Zidane
34. Marcello Lippi
35. Pep Guardiola
36. Carlo Ancelotti
37. Argentina
38. Real Madrid and Bayern Munich
39. Borussia Dortmund and Bayern Munich
40. Monaco and Arsenal
41. Manchester United
42. AC Milan and Juventus
43. Jurgen Klopp
44. AC Milan
45. Liverpool

Round 4: Player Records

46. Can you name the player that has made the most appearances in the Champions League?

47. Which player has scored the most Champions League goals?

48. Who is the oldest player to score a Champions League goal? He did this at 38 years and 59 days.

49. Can you name the player that has received the most yellow cards in this competition?

50. One player has played for a record seven different clubs in the Champions League group stages. Can you name the player?

51. Which player has assisted the most goals in Champions League history?

52. Can you name the player that has scored the most goals in the Champions League group stages?

53. Which player has made the most appearances in the Champions League for one single club?

54. Who was the first player to reach the milestone of making 100 Champions League appearances?

55. Which player has finished as top goal scorer for the most seasons in the competition?

56. Which player has won the most titles? He has lifted the Champions League a record five times.

57. Who is the oldest goalkeeper to win the Champions League?

58. Who is the youngest goalkeeper to win the Champions League?

59. Can you name the oldest ever captain to win the competition?

60. Who is the youngest ever captain to win the competition?

Round 4 Answers

46. Iker Casillas
47. Cristiano Ronaldo
48. Francesco Totti
49. Sergio Ramos
50. Zlatan Ibrahimovic
51. Cristiano Ronaldo
52. Lionel Messi
53. Xavi
54. Raul
55. Cristiano Ronaldo
56. Cristiano Ronaldo
57. Edwin Van der Sar
58. Iker Casillas
59. Paolo Maldini
60. Didier Deschamps

Round 5: Hat-tricks, 4 goals & 5 goals

61. Which two players have scored the most hat-tricks in the competition?

62. Who is the youngest player to have scored a hat-trick in the Champions League? He did this at 18 years and 114 days.

63. Who is the youngest ever player to score a hat-trick on his Champions League debut? He did this at 18 years and 340 days.

64. Who is the oldest ever player to score a hat-trick in the competition?

65. Can you name the two players that have scored five goals in a Champions League match?

66. Who is the only player to score three hat-tricks in the competition in the same season?

67. Can you name the two men that are from the Netherlands, that have scored four goals in a game?

68. One player scored four goals in a Champion League semi-final. Can you name the player?

69. One player scored a hat-trick on his Champions League debut whilst playing for Newcastle United. Can you name the player?

70. One player scored a hat-trick on his Champions League debut whilst playing for Red Bull Salzburg. Can you name the player?

71. Who are the only brothers to have both scored a Champions League hat-trick?

72. Can you name the only person from Cameroon that has scored a hat-trick in the Champions League?

73. Only one French player has scored two Champions League hat-tricks. Who is the player?

74. Can you name the two English players that have scored two hat-tricks in this competition?

75. Can you name the player to score the fastest ever Champions League hat-trick?

Round 5 Answers

61. Cristiano Ronaldo and Lionel Messi
62. Raul
63. Wayne Rooney
64. Cristiano Ronaldo
65. Lionel Messi and Luiz Adriano
66. Cristiano Ronaldo
67. Marco Van Basten and Ruud van Nistlerooy
68. Robert Lewandowski
69. Faustino Asprilla
70. Erling Haland
71. Filippo and Simeone Inzaghi
72. Samuel Eto'o
73. Karim Benzema
74. Andrew Cole and Michael Owen
75. Bafetimbi Gomis

Round 6: Finals

76. Who is the oldest player to score in a Champions League final? He did this at 36 years and 333 days.

77. Who is the youngest player to score in a Champions League final? He did this at 18 years and 327 days.

78. Which player has scored the most goals in Champions League finals?

79. Only one goalkeeper has been sent off in a Champions League final. Who is the goalkeeper?

80. Can you name the two outfield players that have been sent off in a Champions League final?

81. One player holds a record for losing the most Champions League finals. He lost a total of four and three of these were to Barcelona. Who is the player?

82. Two players have scored goals for two different teams in Champions League finals. Can you name the two players?

83. Only one time in the Champions League era was the final settled in extra time. Which two teams were involved in the match and who won after extra time?

84. How many Champions League finals have been settled by a penalty shootout?

85. Only one team has ever scored two goals or more in a Champions League final and still not won the competition. Which team is it?

86. Which player scored Arsenal's only goal in the 2-1 defeat to Barcelona in 2006?

87. Who scored Manchester United's injury time winner in the 1999 final?

88. Who scored Milan's two goals in their 2-1 victory over Liverpool in the 2007 final?

89. Who scored Chelsea's equalizer against Bayern Munich in the 2012 final?

90. Can you name the six Englishmen to score in a Champions League final?

Round 6 Answers

76. Paolo Maldini
77. Patrick Kluivert
78. Cristiano Ronaldo
79. Jens Lehmann
80. Didier Drogba and Juan Cuadrado
81. Patrice Evra
82. Cristiano Ronaldo and Mario Mandzukic
83. Atletico Madrid and Real Madrid (The winners were Real Madrid)
84. Seven
85. AC Milan
86. Sol Campbell
87. Ole Gunnar Solskjaer
88. Filippo Inzaghi
89. Didier Drogba
90. Teddy Sheringham, Steve McManaman, Steven Gerrard, Sol Campbell, Frank Lampard and Wayne Rooney

Round 7: Goalkeepers

91. Can you name the goalkeeper that has made the most appearances without ever winning the competition?

92. Which Brazilian goalkeeper won a Champions League title with Inter Milan?

93. Can you name the two German goalkeepers that have made over 100 appearances in the competition?

94. Can you name the only goalkeeper from the Czech Republic to have made over 100 appearances in the Champions League?

95. Who was Porto´s starting goalkeeper in their Champions League winning final in 2004?

96. Which Liverpool goalkeeper made several mistakes in the 2018 Champions League final?

97. Can you name the goalkeeper that has scored the most goals in Champions League history? The goalkeeper in question has scored three goals in the competition.

98. Which team did Fabien Barthez win the Champions League with?

99. Which Polish goalkeeper started for Liverpool in the 2005 final?

100. Who was the goalkeeper that was on loan from Chelsea that reached and played in the 2014 Champions League final with Atletico Madrid?

101. Can you name the goalkeeper that started the 2019 final as Tottenham Hotspur´s captain?

102. Which Valencia goalkeeper was a losing finalist on two occasions?

103. How many appearances in Champions League finals did AC Milan goalkeeper Dida make?

104. Which three teams did Edwin van der Sar play for in the Champions League?

105. Which three goalkeepers have played in three Champions League finals and won all the three finals?

Round 7 Answers

91. Gianluigi Buffon
92. Julio Cesar
93. Oliver Kahn and Manuel Neuer
94. Petr Cech
95. Vitor Baia
96. Loris Karius
97. Hans-Jorg Butt
98. Marseille
99. Jerzy Dudek
100. Thibaut Courtois
101. Hugo Lloris
102. Santiago Canizares
103. Three
104. Ajax, Juventus and Manchester United
105. Iker Casillas, Victor Valdes and Keylor Navas

Round 8: Defenders

106. Which Brazilian international was a losing finalist with Leverkusen but later went on to win the competition with Inter Milan?

107. Can you name the three English defenders that have made over 100 appearances in the competition?

108. Who is the only German defender to make over 100 appearances in the competition?

109. Which two Brazilian defenders have made over 100 appearances in the competition?

110. Can you name the two Portuguese defenders that won the Champions League with Porto in 2004 that later that summer made a transfer to Chelsea?

111. Which Chelsea defender missed a penalty in the penalty shootout with Manchester United in the 2008 final?

112. Can you name the three Spanish defenders to make over 100 appearances in the Champions League?

113. How many times did Alessandro Nesta win the Champions League?

114. Which defender captained the Real Madrid side that beat Leverkusen in the 2002 final?

115. Can you name Manchester United's two starting centre backs for the 2008 Champions League final?

116. Which Atletico Madrid defender scored the opening goal in the 2014 Champions League final?

117. Which Real Madrid defender scored in both the 2014 and 2016 Champions League finals against Atletico Madrid?

118. Which Mexican international started as a centre back for Barcelona in their 2006 final victory over Arsenal?

119. Can you name the three teams that Ashley Cole made appearances for in the Champions League?

120. Can you name the French defender that won the Champions League with both Marseille and AC Milan?

Round 8 Answers

106. Lucio
107. Gary Neville, Ashley Cole and John Terry
108. Philipp Lahm
109. Roberto Carlos and Dani Alves
110. Ricardo Carvalho and Paulo Ferreira
111. John Terry
112. Carlos Puyol, Gerard Pique and Sergio Ramos
113. Two times
114. Fernando Hierro
115. Rio Ferdinand and Nemanja Vidic
116. Diego Godin
117. Sergio Ramos
118. Rafael Marquez
119. Arsenal, Chelsea and Roma
120. Marcel Desailly

Round 9: Midfielders

121. Can you name the two Manchester United midfielders that were both suspended for the 1999 Champions League final?

122. Which Brazilian midfielder finished top goal scorer in the competition for the 2006-2007 season?

123. How many different teams did David Beckham play for in the competition?

124. Which two teams did Deco win the Champions League with?

125. Can you name the only German midfielder to have made over 100 Champions League appearances?

126. Portuguese legend Figo made a total of 103 appearances in the Champions League. Can you name the three clubs he made these appearances for?

127. Which Czech Republic midfielder missed the 2003 final through suspension? At the time he played for Juventus.

128. Which Valencia midfielder captained his side in both their Champions League final defeats? He also scored in one of the finals.

129. Who was the first Englishman to win the Champions League with two different teams?

130. Which three Liverpool midfielders all scored in the 2005 final?

131. Which Bayern Munich player captained and scored for his team in the 2001 Champions League final?

132. Which player was Chelsea's captain in the 2012 Champions League final?

133. Which Brazilian attacking midfielder player started in the Champions League 2006 final for Barcelona?

134. Can you name the four teams that Wesley Sneijder played for in the Champions League?

135. Can you name the four teams that Xabi Alonso made appearances for in the Champions League?

Round 9 Answers

121. Roy Keane and Paul Scholes
122. Kaka
123. Four teams
124. Porto and Barcelona
125. Toni Kroos
126. Barcelona, Real Madrid and Inter Milan
127. Pavel Nedved
128. Gaizka Mendieta
129. Owen Hargreaves
130. Steven Gerrard, Vladimir Smicer and Xabi Alonso
131. Stefan Effenberg
132. Frank Lampard
133. Ronaldinho
134. Ajax, Real Madrid, Inter Milan and Galatasaray
135. Real Sociedad, Liverpool, Real Madrid and Bayern Munich

Round 10: Forwards

136. Which Brazilian striker started the game for Bayern Munich in the 2001 Champions League final?

137. Only one Juventus player has ever finished as top goal scorer in a Champions League season. Can you name the player?

138. Can you name the two teams that Romario made appearances for in the Champions League?

139. Which Netherlands international finished three seasons as top goal scorer in the competition?

140. Can you name the two French players that have made over 100 appearances in the Champions League?

141. Which forward has made the most appearances for Real Madrid in the Champions League?

142. One striker was the top goal scorer in the competition in the 2003-2004 season whilst on loan at Monaco. Who was the striker?

143. Andriy Shevchenko finished as top goal scorer on two occasions. He did this with two different clubs. Can you name the two teams he achieved this with?

144. Can you name the player that scored two goals for AC Milan in the 2005 Champions League final?

145. An Inter Milan striker scored two goals in the 2010 Champions League final. Who was the player?

146. Which Barcelona forward opened the scoring in the 2011 Champions League final?

147. Three players were joint top goal scorer in the 2014-2015 season. Cristiano Ronaldo and Lionel Messi were two of the players who scored ten goals. Can you name the other player that scored ten goals that season?

148. Who was the first ever striker to score in two Champions League finals for the winning team?

149. Can you name the only forward to come on as a substitute in the Champions League final and score two goals in the game?

150. Which striker won back to back Champions Leagues with different teams in 2009 and 2010?

Round 10 Answers

136. Giovane Elber
137. Alessandro Del Piero
138. PSV and Barcelona
139. Ruud van Nistlerooy
140. Thierry Henry and Karim Benzema
141. Raul
142. Fernando Morientes
143. Dinamo Kyiv and AC Milan
144. Hernan Jorge Crespo
145. Diego Milito
146. Pedro
147. Neymar Jr.
148. Raul
149. Gareth Bale
150. Samuel Eto'o

Round 11: Comebacks

151. Only one team has ever progressed through the knockout phase after losing the first tie 4-0. Can you name the team?

152. In 2004, Liverpool needed a two-goal victory to progress to the knockout stage in their final group stage match. They went 1-0 down in the tie but eventually came back to win 3-1. Who did they play?

153. Manchester United staged an injury time comeback against Bayern Munich in the 1999 Champions League final. What was the final score?

154. Which Tottenham Hotspur player scored a second half hat-trick to complete their comeback against Ajax and take his team to the 2019 Champions League final?

155. AS Roma lost 4-1 in the first leg of their 2018 Champions League quarter final. They won the second leg 3-0 and went through on away goals. Who did they beat?

156. Only one team has ever trailed by three goals in a Champions League final and still managed to win the tie. Can you name the team?

157. Barcelona beat a team 3-0 in the home tie of the 2019 semi-final. They lost the away tie 4-0 and went out of the competition. Which team defeated them over the two legs?

158. One Spanish team came from 3-0 down in a game to win 4-3 against PSG in the 2000-2001 season. Can you name the Spanish team?

159. Which Belgian team came from 3-0 down to draw 3-3-3 against Arsenal during the 2014-2015 group stage?

160. Basel were leading an English team 3-0 in a group stage game during the 2002-2003 season. The English team came back to draw the game 3-3. Can you name the English team?

161. One Spanish team lost a Champions League quarter final first leg 4-1 to AC Milan. In the second leg they won 4-0 to win the tie. This was in the 2003-2004 season. Can you name the Spanish team?

162. One English team surrendered a 3-0 lead to Sevilla during the 2017-2018 group stage. The tie finished 3-3. Can you name the English team?

163. Real Madrid won the home time of their 2004 quarter final 4-2. However, they went out on away goals after losing the away tie 3-1. Which team knocked them out?

164. Can you name the only English team to progress through the group stages after losing their opening three games?

165. Only one team has ever lost the first tie at home by two goals in the knockout phase and still managed to qualify. Can you name the team?

Round 11 Answers

151. Barcelona
152. Olympiakos
153. Manchester United 2-1 Bayern Munich
154. Lucas Moura
155. Barcelona
156. Liverpool
157. Liverpool
158. Deportivo La Coruna
159. Anderlecht
160. Liverpool
161. Deportivo La Coruna
162. Liverpool
163. Monaco
164. Newcastle United
165. Manchester United

Round 12: Amazing Goals

166. Which Real Madrid player scored a left footed volley from a Roberto Carlos looping cross in the 2002 Champions League final?

167. Which player scored a great goal with a few shuffles and then a strike with the outside of his boot? The goal was against Chelsea and was at Stamford Bridge.

168. One Manchester United player scored a fantastic goal from outside the box against Barcelona in the 2008 semi-final second leg. Manchester United won the tie 1-0 on aggregate over the two legs. Can you name the player that scored the goal?

169. Can you name the Chelsea player that scored a tremendous left footed volley from outside the box against Barcelona? This was in the semi-final in the 2008-2009 season.

170. Which Real Madrid player scored an overhead kick against Juventus? This was in Real Madrid's away tie of their 2018 quarter final.

171. Can you name the Serbian player that scored a volley from the halfway line for Inter Milan against Schalke 04?

172. In the 2006 knockout stages, an Arsenal player beat four players and then slotted the ball in with his left foot. This goal was against Real Madrid in the Santiago Bernabeu stadium. Can you name the Arsenal player?

173. One of the best free kicks ever scored in the competition came from a Lyon player in a game against Bayern Munich. Can you name the Lyon player?

174. Can you name the Liverpool player that hit a fantastic strike from outside the box to put his team 3-1 up against Olympiakos? This sent his team through to the knockout stages of the competition.

175. In the 1999-2000 group stage, a Valencia player let a long ball come over his shoulder and timed his volley to perfection and scored against PSV. Can you name the Argentinian player that scored this goal?

176. Can you name the Barcelona player that took on four Real Madrid players before slotting the ball home with his right foot? He did this in a Champions League semi-final in the 2010-2011 season.

177. Which Real Madrid player scored an outstanding overhead kick in the 2018 final against Liverpool?

178. Can you name the Fiorentina player who scored a long-range powerful strike in a tie against Manchester United in the 1999-2000 season?

179. Which Manchester United player scored a 40-yard strike against Porto in the 2009 knockout phase?

180. Which Barcelona player scored an injury time equalizer that took his team through to the 2009 Champions League final at the expense of Chelsea? He scored the goal from outside the box with the outside of his right foot.

Round 12 Answers

166. Zinedine Zidane
167. Ronaldinho
168. Paul Scholes
169. Michael Essien
170. Cristiano Ronaldo
171. Dejan Stankovic
172. Thierry Henry
173. Juninho
174. Steven Gerrard
175. Claudio Lopez
176. Lionel Messi
177. Gareth Bale
178. Gabriel Batistuta
179. Cristiano Ronaldo
180. Andres Iniesta

Round 13: Memorable Moments

181. Which Liverpool player scored the 'Ghost Goal' during a 2005 semi-final with Chelsea?

182. During a game with Barcelona, one Chelsea player chased after the referee after he was not awarded a penalty. Can you name the player that chased after the referee?

183. Which Arsenal player was sent off in a knockout round game with Barcelona in 2011, for supposedly kicking the ball away after the referee had blown his whistle for offside? The player in question, insisted he never heard the whistle.

184. A Manchester City player scored an injury-time goal against Tottenham Hotspur in the 2019 quarter final, and then the goal was overturned by VAR. Can you name the player who had the goal disallowed?

185. Manchester United lost the first leg of a quarter final 2-1 in the 2006-2007 season. They won the second leg 7-1 at Old Trafford. Which team did they beat?

186. At which English stadium did Jose Mourinho celebrate a Porto goal in the Champions League by running down the touchline?

187. Can you name the AC Milan player that put on a fantastic display and scored two goals in an away tie at Old Trafford? The game was the 2007 semi-final and Manchester United won the first leg 3-2.

188. Two English sides played out a quarter final in the 2008-2009 season and the aggregate score was 7-5. Can you name the two teams involved in the quarter final?

189. During a 2008 quarter final, Theo Walcott assisted a goal after running from his own penalty box and beating four players in a game against Liverpool. Which player scored from his assist?

190. Which teenager came on as a substitute and scored a sublime lob for Borussia Dortmund in the 1997 Champions League final?

191. Can you name the Arsenal player that made it 2-1 to Arsenal against Barcelona? This was in the first leg of a knockout phase game in 2010-2011 season?

192. Manchester United came back from 2-0 down to win 3-2 in a Champions League semi-final second leg in the 1998-1999 season. Which team did they stage this comeback against?

193. Borussia Dortmund scored two injury time goals to win a quarter final second leg 3-2 against a Spanish team. This was in the 2012-2013 season. Can you name the Spanish team they beat?

194. Chelsea secured their place in the 2012 final by coming back from 2-0 down in the semi-final despite having a man sent off. Which two players scored their goals?

195. Barcelona lost 4-0 in a round of 16 first leg to PSG in the 2016-2017 season. They came back to win the second leg and progressed to the quarter final. What was the score in the second leg?

Round 13 Answers

181. Luis Garcia
182. Michael Ballack
183. Robin van Persie
184. Raheem Sterling
185. AS Roma
186. Old Trafford
187. Kaka
188. Chelsea and Liverpool
189. Emmanuel Adebayor
190. Lars Ricken
191. Andrey Arshavin
192. Juventus
193. Malaga
194. Ramires and Fernando Torres
195. Barcelona 6-1 PSG

Round 14: Managers 2nd Round

196. Which manager led Chelsea to Champions League glory?

197. Can you name the two Champions League winning managers that have also won the World Cup?

198. Who was Chelsea's manager when they were defeated by Manchester United in the Champions League final in 2008?

199. Who was Monaco's manager when they were losing finalists in 2004?

200. Which manager won the 2013-2014 Champions League with Real Madrid?

201. Which English manager took Tottenham Hotspur to the Champions League in the 2010-2011 season?

202. Who was Ajax's manager when they won the Champions League final in 1995?

203. Which Juventus manager was a losing finalist in both 2015 and 2017?

204. Barcelona won the Champions League in the 2005-2006 season. Who was their manager at the time?

205. Which two teams has Thomas Tuchel managed in the Champions League?

206. Can you name the manager that led Manchester City to the semi-finals of the competition in the 2015-2016 season?

207. Who was Bayern Munich's manager when they lost the 2010 Champions League final?

208. Leeds United reached the Champions League semi-final stage in the 2000-2001 season. Who was their manager during this season?

209. Who was the manager of Barcelona when they lost the 1994 Champions League final to AC Milan?

210. Which English manager took Newcastle United back into the Champions League in the 2002-2003 season?

Round 14 Answers

196. Roberto Di Matteo
197. Vicente del Bosque and Marcello Lippi
198. Avram Grant
199. Didier Deschamps
200. Carlo Ancelotti
201. Harry Redknapp
202. Louis van Gaal
203. Massimiliano Allegri
204. Frank Rijkaard
205. Borussia Dortmund and PSG
206. Manuel Pellegrini
207. Louis van Gaal
208. David O'Leary
209. Johan Cruyff
210. Sir Bobby Robson

Round 15: Final Locations

211. Where was the 1999 final between Manchester United and Bayern Munich held?

212. Liverpool and AC Milan contested the 2005 final. Which city was the game played in?

213. Which city did Manchester United and Chelsea play their 2008 final in?

214. Which team plays their home games where the most recent Champions League final was held in 2019?

215. Which team won the only final to be held in Scotland?

216. Which team won the first final to be hosted at Wembley?

217. Three finals have been held in England. Two were at Wembley. What was the other ground to host a Champions League final?

218. Which city hosted the 2009 final between Barcelona and Manchester United?

219. How many times has the final been at the San Siro, Milan?

220. Arsenal and Barcelona played the 2006 final at a national stadium. Which country plays their home games in that stadium?

221. Which team won the only final to be staged at the Santiago Bernabeu Stadium?

222. Which country was the 2018 final between Liverpool and Real Madrid in?

223. AC Milan and Ajax played in the 1995 final. Which city hosted this final?

224. Only one club has won the Champions League final at the same location two times. Which team is it?

225. Only one club has been involved in a Champions League final that was played at their home ground. Can you name the team?

Round 15 Answers

211. Nou Camp, Barcelona
212. Istanbul
213. Moscow
214. Atletico Madrid
215. Real Madrid
216. Barcelona
217. Old Trafford, Manchester
218. Rome
219. Two times
220. France
221. Inter Milan
222. Ukraine
223. Vienna
224. AC Milan
225. Bayern Munich

Round 16: Defenders 2nd Round

226. There was only one non-German player in the starting line-up for Bayern Munich in their 1999 Champions League final. This player came from an African country. Can you name him?

227. Can you name the English left back that started for Chelsea in advanced left winger role in the 2012 Champions League final?

228. Can you name the left back that started for Liverpool in the 2005 Champions League final?

229. Which two Ivorian defenders started for Arsenal in the 2006 Champions League final?

230. Which right back started both Real Madrid's 2000 and 2002 Champions League final victories?

231. Bayern Munich started the 2001 Champions League final with two French wing backs. Can you name them both?

232. Which two teams did Jaap Stam play in Champions League finals with?

233. Which Brazilian centre back started for Bayern Munich in the 2013 final?

234. Can you name the Netherlands international that started at centre back for Barcelona in the 1994 final?

235. Can you name the Argentinian player that started at centre back for Inter Milan in their 2009 final triumph?

236. Which French international started at centre back for Real Madrid in both their 2017 and 2018 Champions League final wins?

237. Can you name the Norwegian centre back that started for Manchester United in their 1999 final victory?

238. Which Brazilian player started at centre back for Chelsea in the 2012 final?

239. Liverpool started the 2007 final with Jamie Carragher and a Danish player as their centre backs. Can you name the Danish player?

240. Can you name Borussia Dortmund's two starting centre backs in the 2013 Champions League final?

Round 16 Answers

226. Samuel Kuffour
227. Ryan Bertrand
228. Djimi Traore
229. Kolo Toure and Emmanuel Eboue
230. Michel Salgado
231. Bixente Lizarazu and Willy Sagnol
232. Manchester United and AC Milan
233. Dante
234. Ronald Koeman
235. Walter Samuel
236. Raphael Varane
237. Ronny Johnsen
238. David Luiz
239. Daniel Agger
240. Mats Hummels and Neven Subotic

Round 17: Midfielders 2nd Round

241. Can you name the only player from Israel that has scored a hat-trick in the Champions League?

242. Which two teams did Bastian Schweinsteiger play for in the Champions League?

243. Can you name the Barcelona midfielder that started the 2009 final against Manchester United as a centre back?

244. Which Borussia Dortmund midfielder scored a goal from the penalty spot in the 2013 final?

245. Which midfielder captained his Barcelona side to victory in the 2015 final?

246. Can you name the only Real Madrid midfielder that started all the Champions League finals in 2014, 2016, 2017 and 2018?

247. Which Argentinian captained the Real Madrid side that won the 2000 final?

248. Can you name the Portuguese international that played in the 2003 final for AC Milan?

249. Which two teams did Edgar Davids lose Champions League finals with?

250. Which team did Mark van Bommel win the Champions League with?

251. Which Argentinian player captained Inter Milan in their 2010 Champions League win?

252. Can you name the only Scottish player in the Borussia Dortmund starting line-up in the 1997 Champions League final?

253. Which Swedish player started for Manchester United in the 1999 final?

254. Which Brazilian midfielder started for Liverpool in the 2019 final?

255. Can you name the Barcelona player that opened the scoring in the 2015 final?

Round 17 Answers

241. Yossi Benayoun
242. Bayern Munich and Manchester United
243. Yaya Toure
244. Ilkay Gundogan
245. Andres Iniesta
246. Luka Modric
247. Fernando Redondo
248. Rui Costa
249. Ajax and Juventus
250. Barcelona
251. Javier Zanetti
252. Paul Lambert
253. Jesper Blomqvist
254. Fabinho
255. Ivan Rakitic

Round 18: Forwards 2nd Round

256. Can you name the team that Gareth Bale scored a second half hat-trick against in the Champions League?

257. Which striker scored Liverpool's late consolation goal in the 2007 Champions League final against AC Milan?

258. Which club did John Carew play for in a Champions League final?

259. Can you name the two French strikers that have scored a Champions League hat-trick for Arsenal?

260. Brazilian legend Ronaldo scored only one hat-trick in the Champions League. Can you name the team he scored the hat-trick against?

261. Which Brazilian forward finished as joint top goal scorer in the 1999-2000 season?

262. Can you name the two teams that Gabriel Batistuta played for in the Champions League?

263. Which Borussia Dortmund striker scored two goals in the 1997 Champions League final?

264. Can you name the German striker that started the 1999 final as Bayern Munich's central forward?

265. Can you name the two Manchester United strikers that scored in the 3-2 semi-final comeback against Juventus?

266. Lionel Messi and Pedro both scored in Barcelona's 2011 Champions League final win over Manchester United? Who scored the other goal for Barcelona?

267. Only one player has scored a hat-trick for Blackburn Rovers in the competition. Can you name him?

268. Can you name the only Juventus player that scored in the 2015 Champions League final?

269. Which Italian striker opened the scoring for Juventus in the 1996 Champions League final?

270. Can you name the player that has scored a hat-trick for both Bayern Munich and Deportivo La Coruna in the Champions League?

Round 18 Answers

256. Inter Milan
257. Dirk Kuyt
258. Valencia
259. Thierry Henry and Olivier Giroud
260. Manchester United
261. Rivaldo
262. Fiorentina and AS Roma
263. Karl-Heinz Riedle
264. Carston Jancker
265. Andy Cole and Dwight Yorke
266. David Villa
267. Mike Newell
268. Alvaro Morata
269. Fabrizio Ravanelli
270. Roy Makaay

Round 19: Penalty Shootout Trivia

271. Only one Manchester United player missed in the penalty shootout in the 2008 final. Can you name him?

272. Which player missed AC Milan's last penalty in the 2005 final?

273. Which striker missed Juventus' first penalty in the 2003 final?

274. John Terry missed a penalty in the 2008 final. Who was the other Chelsea player to miss a penalty?

275. Can you name the Chelsea player that scored the winning and decisive last penalty in the 2012 final?

276. Can you name the Real Madrid player that scored the winning and decisive last penalty in the 2016 final?

277. Only one Liverpool player missed his penalty in the 2005 final. Can you name the player?

278. Which Juventus goalkeeper saved two penalties in the 1996 Champions League final?

279. Can you name the Spanish player that missed Chelsea's opening penalty in the 2012 Champions League final?

280. Can you name the two English players that took penalties for Manchester United in the 2008 final? Both players scored their penalties.

281. Which German player missed his penalty for Bayern Munich in the 2012 final?

282. Can you name the Ajax player that stepped up and took the first penalty in the 1996 final shootout? The player in question, missed his penalty.

283. Which Liverpool striker scored a penalty in the 2005 final shootout?

284. Can you name the only team in a Champions League final to score 5 out of 5 penalties in a shootout?

285. Can you name the only goalkeeper to take a penalty in a Champions League final? The goalkeeper in question, scored his penalty.

Round 19 Answers

271. Cristiano Ronaldo
272. Andriy Shevchenko
273. David Trezeguet
274. Nicolas Anelka
275. Didier Drogba
276. Cristiano Ronaldo
277. John Arne Riise
278. Angelo Peruzzi
279. Juan Mata
280. Michael Carrick and Owen Hargreaves
281. Bastian Schweinsteiger
282. Edgar Davids
283. Djibril Cisse
284. Real Madrid
285. Manuel Neuer

Round 20: Challenging Trivia

286. Only one set of brothers have ever started a Champions League final together. Can you name them?

287. Who is the only player to reach four Champions League quarter finals with four different clubs? He is a midfielder.

288. Who is the only Finnish player to ever be top goal scorer in a Champions League season?

289. Only one Peruvian player has scored a hat-trick in the Champions League. Can you name him?

290. Which Spanish player has scored the most Champions League hat-tricks?

291. George Weah finished one season as the top goal scorer in the Champions League with seven goals. Which team was he playing for when he achieved this?

292. Only one Uruguayan player has scored a Champions League hat-trick. Can you name the player?

293. Only one Danish player has scored a Champions League hat-trick. Can you name the player?

294. Which player has been sent off for three different teams in the Champions League?

295. Who are the only two people to have won the Champions League as a player and then later go on to win the competition as a manager?

296. Who are the three teams that have reached three consecutive finals in the Champions League?

297. Which club hold the record for the most consecutive clean sheets in the competition? They kept a record consecutive 10 clean sheets.

298. Only one club has ever played in a Champions League final that has never won their own domestic league. Can you name the team?

299. Only one team have been unbeaten throughout the competition two times in the Champions League era. Which team is it?

300. Who is the only player to have won the Champions League with three different teams?

Round 20 Answers

286. Frank de Boer and Ronald de Boer
287. Michael Ballack
288. Jari Litmanen
289. Claudio Pizarro
290. Roberto Soldado
291. PSG
292. Walter Pandiani
293. Nicklas Bendtner
294. Patrick Vieira
295. Frank Rijkaard and Zinedine Zidane
296. AC Milan, Juventus and Real Madrid
297. Arsenal
298. Bayer 04 Leverkusen
299. Manchester United
300. Clarence Seedorf

Congratulations!

You have completed all 20 rounds of the UEFA Champions League Quiz.

There will be more quiz books coming your way soon by QuizGuy, so please keep this in mind. Please find the details of another quiz book by QuizGuy on the next page.

One last thing.........

If you have enjoyed the quiz book, please write a review about this publication. This is helpful for the author and it will provide useful feedback.

Other work by QuizGuy.

Printed in Great Britain
by Amazon